NUCLEAR ENERGY

To my children
Christopher and Andrea

Library of Congress Number: 82-9790

Printed and bound in the United States of America.

1234567890   8786858483

Library of Congress Cataloging in Publication Data

Coble, Charles R.
  Nuclear energy.

  (A Look inside)
  Includes index.
  SUMMARY: A history of nuclear energy, describing fission and fusion, safety aspects of nuclear reactors, and the future of this potent source of power.
    1. Atomic power — Juvenile literature.
2. Atomic energy — Juvenile literature. [1. Atomic energy. 2. Atomic power] I. Title. II. Series.
TK9148.C6   1982   621.48   82-9790
ISBN 0-8172-1416-X   AACR2

21118018M

TS   25.25

NUCLEAR ENERGY

By Charles Coble

CONTENTS

RAINTREE PUBLISHERS
Milwaukee · Toronto · Mexico City · London

A NEW SOURCE OF ENERGY

Energy is necessary for life. Without it, no work could be done. Over the ages people have learned to do more and more work by using energy beyond the strength of their own muscles. Societies that have used their sources of energy well have prospered.

During the last 100 years, we have used much more energy than ever before. We have also changed our energy sources. Wood was the most common source of energy in the United States until it was overtaken by coal in about 1890. In 1950, oil surpassed coal. Natural gas has also given us large amounts of energy in the last 30 years, although natural gas production peaked in 1973.

In the 1960s, we began to use a new source of energy. This new source of energy was more powerful than any other source ever used. Yet, it came from a very tiny particle of matter — the nucleus of an atom. At first it was called atomic energy, but now we

call it nuclear energy. Nuclear energy is the energy released by changes in the nucleus of an atom. In order to understand nuclear energy, you have to know some things about atoms.

ATOMS AND ELEMENTS

Atoms are the "building blocks" of all matter: solids, liquids, and gases. There are 90 kinds of naturally occurring atoms. These atoms make up the 90 naturally occurring elements, such as oxygen, carbon, iron, and so on. Scientists have made at least 14 other artificial elements in controlled experiments on earth.

Atoms are made up of smaller atomic particles, called protons, neutrons and electrons. Protons are particles that have a positive electrical charge. Neutrons are particles with no electrical charge. Protons and neutrons make up the nucleus, the center, of the atom. Only one element is different: normal hydrogen atoms have only one proton and no neutrons in the nucleus.

The nucleus of every atom is surrounded by a "cloud" of electrons. Electrons are particles that have a negative electrical charge. The number of protons inside the nucleus is usually the same as the number of electrons outside the nucleus. Therefore, an atom is normally neutral; that is, it has a balanced electrical charge.

Each kind of atom has a certain number of protons in its nucleus. This number of protons is called the *atomic number.* For example, all atoms that have only one proton in the nucleus are hydrogen atoms. Thus, hydrogen atoms have an atomic number of 1. All atoms that have eight protons in the nucleus are oxygen atoms. The atomic number of oxygen is 8.

The nucleus holds almost all the mass of an atom. (Mass is a measure of how much matter is in an object. It's just like weight, except it can be measured even in places where there is no gravity.) The total number of protons and neutrons in an atom is called the

The carbon 14 isotope (above) has 6 protons and 8 neutrons in the nucleus. A normal carbon 12 atom (below) has 6 protons and 6 neutrons. Both atoms have 6 electrons.

7

mass number of that atom. For example, most oxygen atoms have eight protons and eight neutrons. Thus, the mass number of oxygen is 16.

Although the number of protons in an atom of an element is always the same, the number of neutrons may vary. All carbon atoms have six protons. They usually have six neutrons. However, some carbon atoms have eight neutrons. Atoms that have the same number of protons, but different numbers of neutrons, are called *isotopes.* The most common form of carbon is carbon 12. It has six protons and six neutrons and a mass number of 12. The isotope of carbon with eight neutrons would be called carbon 14, because its mass number would be 14 (six protons and eight neutrons).

Another element with isotopes is uranium. Uranium has an atomic number of 92, which is the number of protons in its nucleus. Two of its common isotopes are uranium 238 and uranium 235. Uranium 238 (U-238) has 146 neutrons. Uranium 235 (U-235) has 143 neutrons. The two isotopes of uranium play an important role in the story of nuclear energy.

RADIATION

Most atoms in nature do not change. They keep their original structure, with a fixed number of protons, neutrons and electrons. They don't normally release energy and light. They make up elements that are considered stable.

However, a few elements are naturally unstable. For example, if you put a chunk of uranium on a sheet of color negative film in the dark for several hours, it would "take its own picture." The film is exposed because uranium is unstable — it is *radioactive.* That is how radioactivity was discovered by the French scientist, Henri Becquerel, in 1896.

Radioactivity is a release of energy due to changes in the nuclei of atoms. (Nuclei is the plural of

This is a uranium 235 atom. It has 92 protons, 143 neutrons and 92 electrons.

Diane Christensen

nucleus.) Radioactivity usually occurs in atoms heavier than lead. However, some of the isotopes of lighter elements are also radioactive. For example, certain isotopes of carbon and potassium are radioactive. You have a small amount of these isotopes in your body.

Around the turn of the century, Professor Ernest Rutherford in England sent a beam of radiation from uranium toward a piece of photographic film. The beam passed between the poles of a magnet. The magnet split the beam into three parts which made three spots on the film.

This and other studies showed that natural radiation is made up of three main types of particles, called alpha, beta, and gamma radiation.

Alpha radiation is made up of positively charged particles, called alpha particles. Beta radiation is made up of negatively charged particles, called beta particles. Gamma radiation is made up of waves of energy. Gamma rays are like X rays.

All radiation can hurt living cells and tissues. If the damage is bad enough, this causes radiation sickness, which can be fatal. People working with radioactive elements are cautious. They shield themselves and others from radiation.

Uranium and other radioactive elements can be found with a tool called a Geiger counter. The invisible radiation sets off an electrical charge in the counter. This causes the counter to make a clicking sound. The "richer" the radioactive content of the element, the more clicks come from the Geiger counter.

RADIOACTIVE DECAY AND HALF-LIFE

The French scientists Marie and Pierre Curie also studied uranium at the turn of the century. They discovered that the nuclei of some radioactive elements break apart. The breaking up of the nucleus is called *radioactive decay*. As elements undergo radioactive decay, they change into isotopes of other elements, which may also change. Most radioactive elements give off gamma rays when they decay. Some also give off alpha particles, and some give off beta

particles. Some radioactive elements give off all three.

Radioactive material decays at a certain rate. A measurement of this time is called half-life. Half-life is the time it takes for half of the atoms in a radioactive material to decay. The half-life of uranium 238 is about 4.5 billion years. This means that in 4.5 billion years, 1 gram of uranium 238 decays to 0.5 gram. The shorter the half-life of an element, the more radioactive the isotope.

Radioactivity in nature is important. Without it, scientists would never have achieved the amazing feat of splitting the nucleus of the atom and using its power. Doctors also use radioactivity to find and cure illnesses.

Marie Curie is shown in a photograph that was taken shortly before her death in 1934.

NUCLEAR ENERGY RELEASED

In 1905, Albert Einstein stated a remarkable theory: that matter and energy were equivalent to each other. This meant that matter could be converted to energy. The amount of energy (E) produced would be equal to a given mass of matter (M) destroyed, multiplied by the speed of light (C) multiplied by itself (squared). His famous equation looked like this: $E = MC^2$.

Einstein's equation explained why atoms, so small that half a million of them might be in the period at the end of this sentence, could explode into so much energy. His theory was proved in 1932, when a giant "atom-smasher" released a tremendous burst of energy from a lithium atom.

In January 1939, German scientists discovered that they could split the nuclei of the atoms of uranium 235. The loss of mass was far greater than in any previous atom-smashing experiment. The release of energy was also astounding — 200,000,000 electron

Albert Einstein (1879 - 1955)

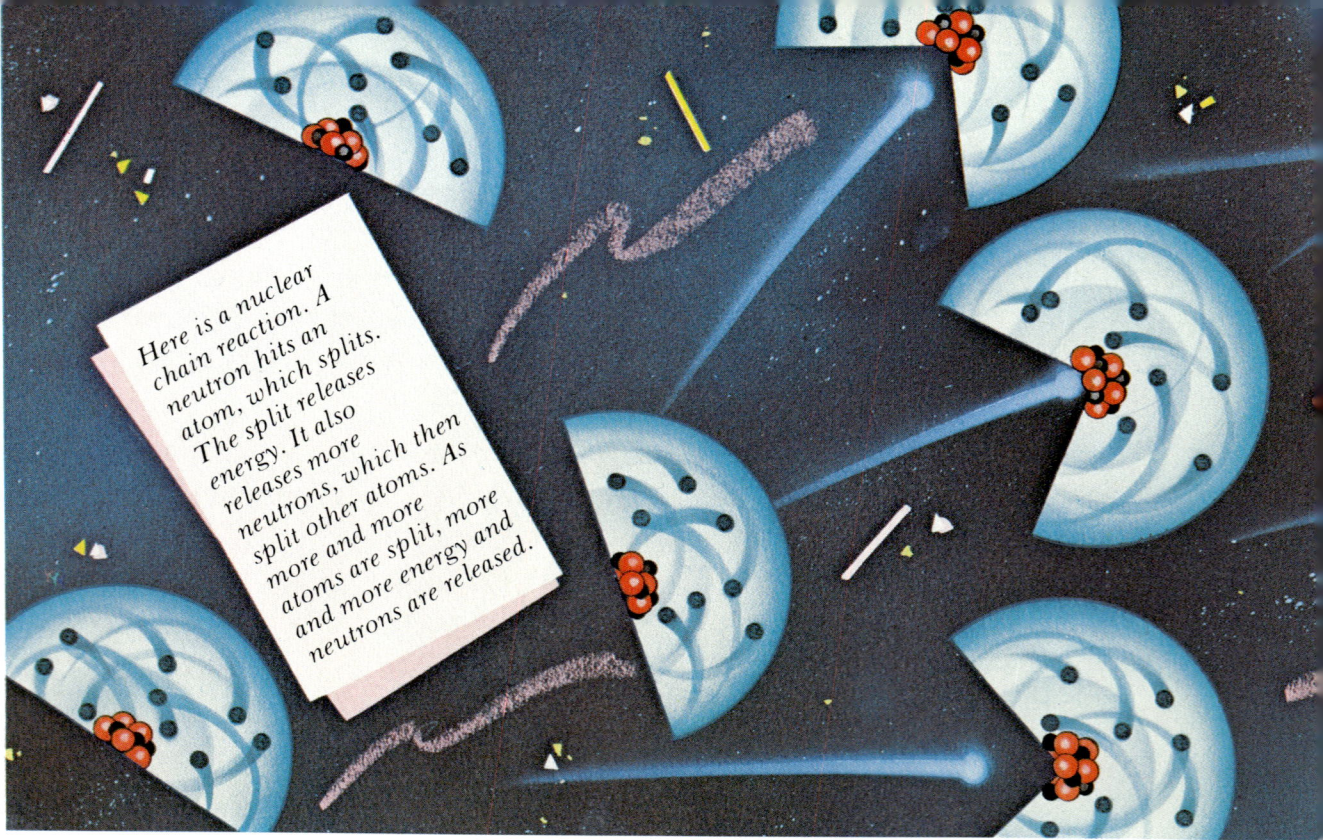

Here is a nuclear chain reaction. A neutron hits an atom, which splits. The split releases energy. It also releases more neutrons, which then split other atoms. As more and more atoms are split, more and more energy and neutrons are released.

volts. (Electron volts are standard units for measuring electrical energy.)

This discovery came at the beginning of World War II. Many scientists were forced to leave Europe. One of them, Dr. Niels Bohr, flew to the United States to discuss the new discovery with Einstein. A group of scientists decided to call the splitting of the uranium 235 atom "fission." Fission means division. In nu-clear fission, one nucleus is split into two or more lighter nuclei. Those nuclei have less mass than the original nucleus. The lost mass becomes energy in the form of heat and radiation.

Only certain radioactive isotopes, like uranium 235, will split when struck by neutrons. During nuclear fission a neutron from one atom combines with the nucleus of a uranium 235 atom, causing it to split (fission). This

Diane Christensen

usually releases other neutrons. These neutrons cause more uranium atoms to split, releasing still more neutrons, which may then split more uranium 235 nuclei, which free more neutrons. The fission of nuclei and release of neutrons goes on, causing a chain reaction. A chain reaction is a series of events where one event makes the next one happen, which makes the next one happen, and so on. A nuclear chain reaction releases a huge amount of energy.

The scientists who were studying fission realized that the energy released by a fission reaction could be developed into a weapon. Dr. Einstein sent a secret letter to President Roosevelt explaining the importance of their discovery. The President decided to put together a massive effort to develop a new weapon to help win the war against

Germany and Japan.

The scientists knew that just the right amount, a "critical mass," of uranium 235 had to be present before a chain reaction could begin. The problem was to find out what that critical mass was. They discovered that if pellets of uranium 235 were held in blocks of graphite, they could more easily control the speed of the chain reaction. They began to build a pile of graphite blocks, some containing uranium 235. Cadmium rods were put into the pile. Cadmium is a metal that can absorb neutrons. Cadmium rods can stop a chain reaction.

The pile was built under the west stands of Stagg Field at the University of Chicago. By December 2, 1942, the scientists had built about seven tons of uranium metal into the pile. As the cadmium rods were raised, the Geiger counters began to go wild, and

This painting shows the site at the University of Chicago where the first controlled chain reaction took place, in December 1942.

heat began to build rapidly. All instruments showed that a chain reaction had begun. They immediately lowered the rods and stopped the reaction. For the first time, it was proven that energy from an atom could be released and controlled. The world had entered a new era.

The first use of this knowledge was an atomic bomb. Scientists worked out a way to load a bomb with a type of gun which shot half the critical mass of uranium into the other half.

The first atomic bomb was exploded in a controlled test on July 16, 1945, in the desert of southeastern New Mexico. Only 21 days later, the United States dropped an atomic bomb on Hiroshima, Japan. The bomb had the power of 20,000 tons of dynamite. Nearly 100,000 people were killed in Hiroshima. Three days later a second atomic bomb was dropped on the naval base of Nagasaki, Japan. Five days later the Japanese surrendered.

The United States Congress moved control of the U.S. Atomic Energy Program from the military to the new civilian Atomic Energy Commission (AEC). Scientists began working to develop peaceful uses of atomic energy. A great deal of attention was given to developing a controlled source of power from nuclear fission. Soon the AEC, working with utility companies, developed ways to produce electricity from nuclear fission.

Several days after two atomic bombs were dropped on Japan, World War II ended.

ELECTRICITY FROM FISSION

Most electricity is fueled by coal, oil, and natural gas. These are called fossil fuels because they were made millions of years ago from ancient plants and animals. In fossil fuel power plants, the fuel is burned to make heat. The heat is sent to a boiler to make steam, and the steam runs a turbine to produce electricity.

The reactor in a nuclear power plant does the same thing that a boiler does in a fossil fuel plant — it produces heat. The process that produces the heat is the fissioning of uranium 235.

Uranium 235 is the fuel in a nuclear power plant. Pure uranium is a white metal more massive than lead. Rocks that hold uranium are fairly common. However, the uranium in most rock is so thinly scattered that it is very hard to get out. The United States has about one-fourth of the world's useful supply of uranium. It is found mainly in New Mexico, Wyoming, Colorado, and Utah. Canada and Zaire also have large deposits.

A nuclear power plant in California.

Uranium is actually a mixture of the two isotopes U-238 and U-235. Only U-235 can be used directly for nuclear power. So the two isotopes have to be separated. Only about seven tenths of one percent of natural uranium is U-235. The problem of sorting out U-235 from U-238 atoms is like finding and removing 7 good apples from 993 bad ones. But it is even more difficult.

First, after mining, the uranium ore is heated to a gas. The the gas is given an electrical charge. Next, the electrically charged gas is sent through a small hole between the poles of a powerful magnet. The magnet pulls at the atoms. But the more massive U-238 atoms are not pulled quite as sharply as the atoms of U-235. The result is that the atoms separate and are collected into different areas.

There are other methods of separating U-238 and U-235. Almost all of them rely on the difference in mass of the two isotopes of uranium.

The core of the reactor contains the uranium fuel. A mixture of about 3% U-235 and 97% U-238 is formed into pellets. The pellets are about 1¼ centimeters (½ in) wide and 2½ centimeters (1 in) long. They are stacked end-to-end in hollow tubes called fuel rods. The fuel rods are 3½ to 4 meters (12 to 14 ft) long. The fuel rods are put together in bundles, or fuel assemblies. About 200 fuel assemblies are then grouped together to make up the reactor core.

Some of the fuel assemblies contain control rods. They are made of materials that absorb neutrons, stopping them from splitting U-235 atoms. As they are raised from the core the fission process speeds up. When they are lowered into the core, the chain reaction slows down.

The fuel assemblies are arranged so that water or other

At the right is an experimental nuclear reactor in the USSR.

Shown above is the core of an advanced test reactor (ATR).

cool liquids can flow between them. The liquid helps prevent the core from becoming too hot, and helps to control the fission process. If the neutrons which split an atom were going too fast, they would skip over the atoms and fission would not occur. Water slows neutrons down so fission can take place. If water were lost from a reactor by an accident, the chain reaction would stop. However, the reactor core could get very hot, and possibly melt. This could release radioactivity into the air.

TYPES OF NUCLEAR REACTORS

Two main types of nuclear reactors are used to generate electricity around the world today: heavy-water and light-water reactors. Canada, India, Pakistan and some other countries have built heavy-water nuclear reactors. Heavy water is water that is produced by combining deuterium, an isotope of hydrogen, with oxygen. It looks and tastes like ordinary water, but it is heavier.

The nucleus of an ordinary hydrogen atom contains one proton. Deuterium has one proton and one neutron. There is only about 1 deuterium atom for every 5,000 regular hydrogen atoms. It is expensive to separate. So why would anyone want to build a heavy-water reactor? Because heavy water is better for cooling and controlling nuclear

Here are two nuclear generating stations in Pickering, Ontario, Canada.

reactions. Heavy-water reactors can use U-235 more efficiently than light-water reactors. Since uranium is scarce, most countries need the efficiency of the heavy-water reactors.

Because there is a lot of uranium in America, the United States developed light-water nuclear reactors. There are two main types of light-water reactors: the boiling water reactor and the pressurized water reactor. Boiling water reactors heat water in the core and allow the water to boil into steam. The steam goes directly to the turbine outside the reactor. The steam turns the turbine, and this generates electricity.

In a pressurized water reactor, water is kept under pressure to keep it from boiling, even at 300° C (572° F). The pressurized

23

water is pumped through a closed system of pipes called the primary system. Heat from the primary system warms up water in another system, called the secondary system. The secondary system water comes to a boil, and its steam turns the turbine. The primary system water, having given up some of its heat, returns to the reactor vessel.

In both types of reactors, as in all steam-powered electric plants, a separate system draws water from a nearby lake, river, or cooling tower. This cools the exhausted steam back to water.

Nuclear energy was first used to generate electricity in 1951, at the Experimental Breeder Reactor in Idaho Falls, Idaho. In 1954, the United States Navy launched the first nuclear-powered submarine, the *Nautilus*. Modern nuclear-powered submarines are able to stay underwater much longer than the old diesel-powered submarines.

The amount of electricity generated by nuclear energy grew rapidly during the 1960s and early 1970s. By 1981, there were 251 nuclear power plants working worldwide, 74 in the United States. About 13% of the electricity in the U.S. was being generated by nuclear power.

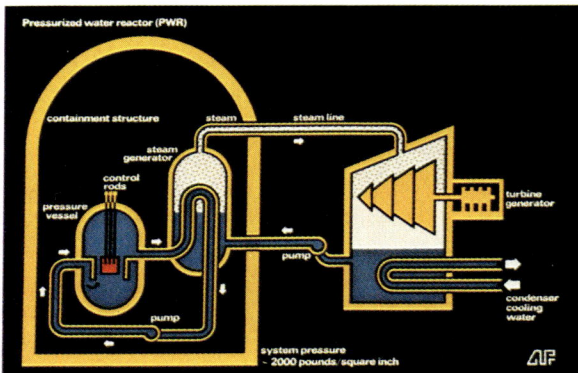

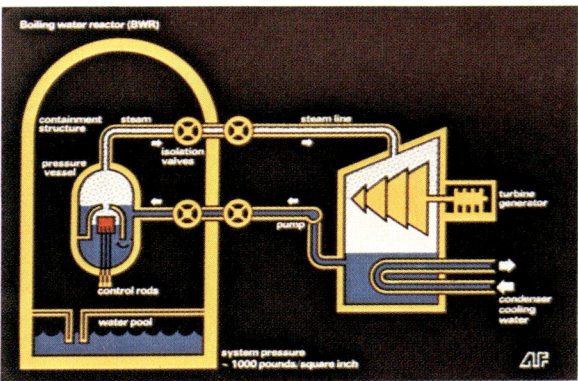

Atomic Industrial Forum

The photo at the left shows containment structures at a nuclear power plant. The diagrams above show two ways that steam can be produced in a nuclear power plant. In both cases, the steam runs a turbine, which in turn generates electricity.

25

NUCLEAR REACTOR SAFETY

U.S. Department of Energy

The manipulator crane at the left is removing an assembly that contains used nuclear fuel. The used fuel will be stored at the nuclear power plant.

Many people fear nuclear power plants because they associate them with atomic bombs. However, U-235 in a nuclear reactor cannot reach critical mass and explode like a bomb. The fission process in a reactor does produce radioactive materials, though, which could be dangerous. The workers keep track of these materials inside and outside the plant. Also, controls to prevent the release of radioactivity are built into every nuclear power plant. Here are some of them:

1. The uranium is formed into ceramic pellets which seal in the radioactive material.

2. The fuel pellets are packed into special zirconium rods which also act as a barrier against the release of radioactivity.

3. The core is placed in a shielded steel reactor vessel whose walls are about 20 centimeters (8 in) thick.

4. The reactor vessel is behind thick concrete walls.

5. All of those things are housed in an airtight building

made of steel-reinforced concrete about 1 meter (3 ft) thick.

6. An emergency core cooling system can pump thousands of gallons of reserve water into the reactor if the pressurized water supply drops.

7. The reactor is operated by remote controls from a central control room located in another building.

8. In addition to human workers, reactors have automatic controls. The controls will shut down the reactor when they detect a change from normal working conditions.

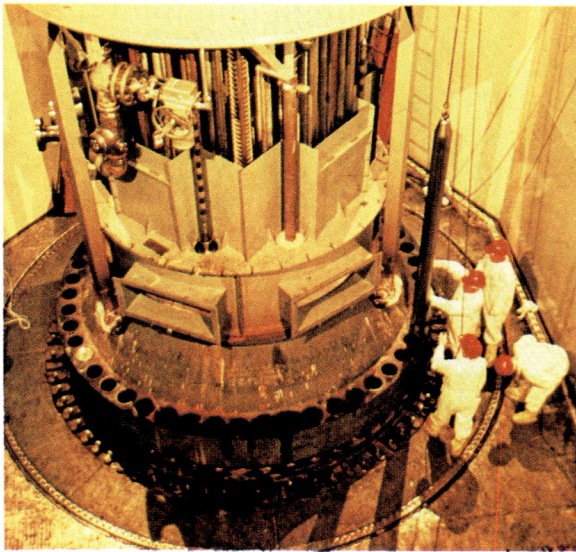

The core of a nuclear reactor.

Westinghouse Corporation

9. A second control room on new plants makes it possible to shut down reactors by hand from outside the central control room.

Unfortunately, safety systems are only as good as the people who run them. They can be turned off, and workers can make mistakes. These controls try to make up for that as much as possible.

Some low-level radioactivity is normally released into the environment. The amount of radiation from nuclear power plants is very low. You get more radiation from natural sources — in food, rock, soil, air, and water. The average person in the U.S. receives around 130 millirems of natural radiation a year. (A millirem is a unit of radiation exposure.) The additional exposure to people living within 80 kilometers of a nuclear power plant is less than 1 millirem per year. However, there are concerns about exposure to radiation from other aspects of nuclear power, such as mining the uranium and

The technician above is using television monitors to inspect the fuel assembly in a nuclear power plant for defects such as deformation.

disposing of nuclear waste.

Two accidents in nuclear power plants have also raised questions about their safety. The first accident took place on October 10, 1957, in the Windscale nuclear reactor on the west coast of England. The reactor caught fire,

The Three Mile Island nuclear power plant in Middletown, Pennsylvania.

and on October 11 was cooled with water. A cloud of radioactive steam rose from the reactor and was carried by the wind over England, Belgium and other countries of Europe. No effects from this have been seen yet, but some scientists think that 10 to 20 people may die of cancer from this radiation by the year 2000.

Most people had forgotten about this accident by March 28, 1979, when several water pumps stopped working in the Unit 1 Nuclear Power Plant on Three Mile Island, near Harrisburg, Pennsylvania. In the minutes, hours and days that followed, a

series of events involving equipment failure and human error resulted in a major accident. When the pumps stopped working, reactor coolant was lost. The core overheated, and the fuel was damaged. Some radioactive gases escaped. The reactor stopped working.

No one was injured or killed. The amount of radiation released was about one thousand times less than at the Windscale accident. However, many people were frightened by how easily the accident seemed to happen. Following the accident, the President and Congress asked the

Nuclear Regulatory Commission (the new name of the Atomic Energy Commission) to develop better safety procedures for nuclear power plants.

NUCLEAR WASTES

Though the burning of fossil fuels and nuclear fission are very different reactions, they both produce wastes. In a nuclear reactor, radioactive isotopes are created during fission. As these fission products begin to build up in the fuel rods, they absorb neutrons. This absorption slowly makes the reactor less efficient. Each year from one-fourth to one-third of the fuel assemblies have to be replaced with fresh fuel. The used fuel is stored underwater in specially designed storage ponds. Some of the radioactive isotopes, such as hydrogen, strontium, iodine, and cesium, are very radioactive and are considered high-level waste. Plutonium and unused uranium will also be left over from the fission process.

Some of the radioactive wastes of nuclear power plants have very short half-lives. They decay to stable, non-radioactive elements in seconds, minutes, hours, or days. A few, however, have very long half-lives and so have to be kept safely from entering the environment for a long time.

Radioactive strontium 90 and cesium 137 have half-lives of around 30 years. A small percent of plutonium 239 is also present, but its half-life is over 24,000 years. These wastes have to be kept away from people and the environment for thousands of years. Plans have been proposed to store highly radioactive wastes in stable areas of land, like underground salt beds. Uranium and plutonium might also be re-used in nuclear plants. However, many people are worried about the safety of these wastes for such a long time. They are afraid that dangerous radioactivity will escape. Adding to this concern is the fact that plutonium could be used to develop nuclear weapons.

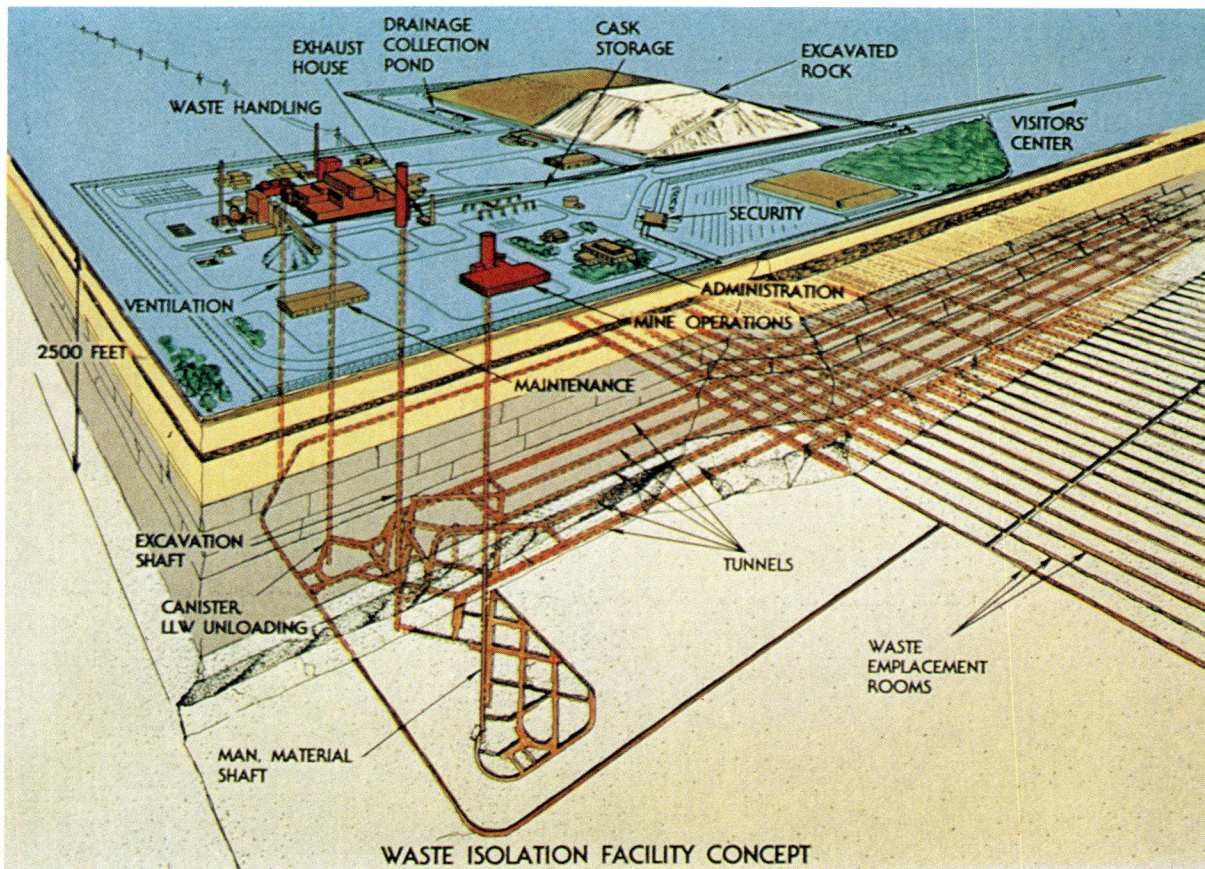

WASTE ISOLATION FACILITY CONCEPT

Labels in the drawing:

- DRAINAGE COLLECTION POND
- EXHAUST HOUSE
- CASK STORAGE
- EXCAVATED ROCK
- WASTE HANDLING
- VISITORS' CENTER
- SECURITY
- VENTILATION
- ADMINISTRATION
- MINE OPERATIONS
- 2500 FEET
- MAINTENANCE
- EXCAVATION SHAFT
- TUNNELS
- CANISTER LLW UNLOADING
- WASTE EMPLACEMENT ROOMS
- MAN, MATERIAL SHAFT

*This is a drawing of a National Waste Terminal
Storage (NWTS) facility. The NWTS is a
research project to develop a safe way to dispose
of radioactive nuclear waste.*

FUSION

Another source of nuclear energy is nuclear fusion. Fusion means to join things together. In nuclear fusion two or more atomic nuclei unite to form a single nucleus and release energy. The energy from the sun comes from fusion reactions.

For nuclear fusion to occur, temperatures must reach millions of degrees Celsius. The temperature inside the sun is about 20 million °C. This is hot enough for hydrogen nuclei to fuse, forming helium atoms. The helium atoms have about 1% less mass than the hydrogen atoms. The lost mass becomes energy, according to Einstein's equation, $E = MC^2$. About 25 million electron volts of energy are freed in the fusion of four hydrogen nuclei in the sun.

Scientists and engineers in many different countries are trying to control the energy released from nuclear fusion. However, it is still hard to do this. Two isotopes of hydrogen, deuterium and tritium, are the most practical fusion fuels. Deuterium can

This photograph of the sun was taken through a solar telescope from Skylab.

be taken from water. Tritium can be made from the element lithium. Deuterium and tritium can be fused to form helium and release energy. The energy could provide the heat to generate electricity in a fusion plant. The heat would be used to make steam to power a turbine generator.

Fusion needs very high temperatures. At these temperatures, in the millions of degrees, atoms are stripped of their electrons. Atoms as such no longer exist. This phase of matter is known as *plasma*. Plasma consists of nuclei and free electrons. If enough of the plasma can be held together long enough at the high temperature needed, the fuel will fuse to release vast amounts of energy.

The most promising method

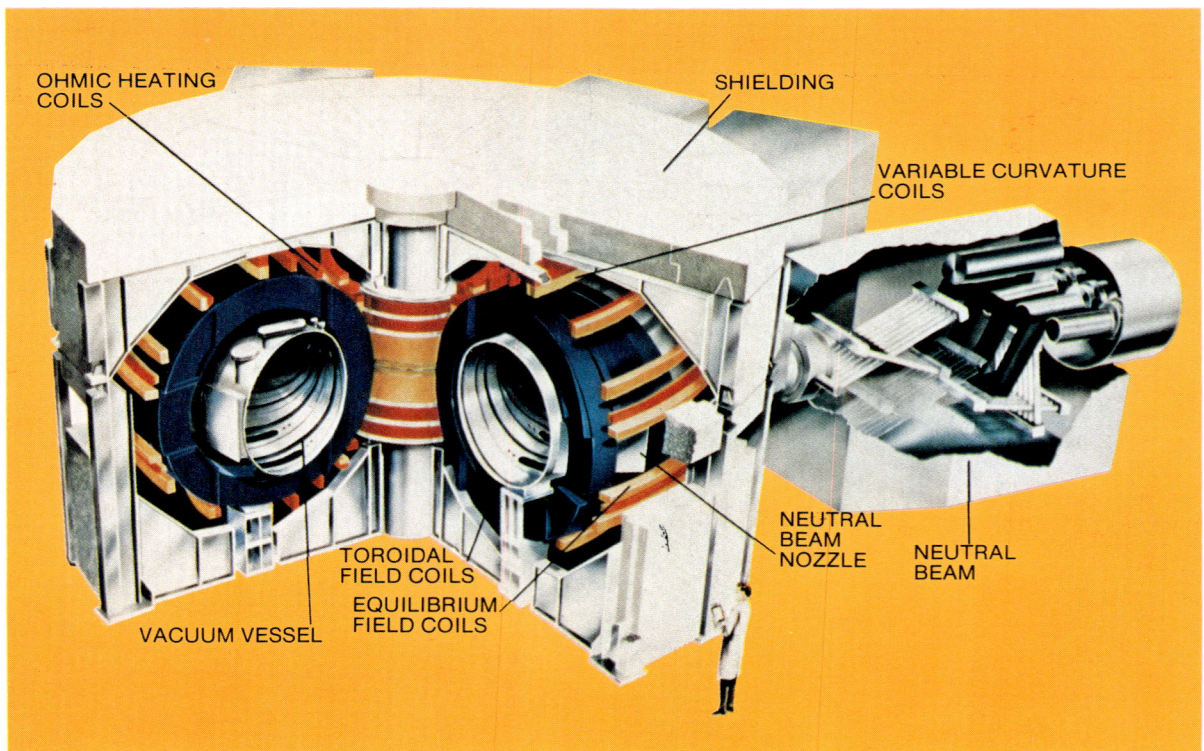

OHMIC HEATING COILS

SHIELDING

VARIABLE CURVATURE COILS

NEUTRAL BEAM NOZZLE

NEUTRAL BEAM

TOROIDAL FIELD COILS

EQUILIBRIUM FIELD COILS

VACUUM VESSEL

for achieving power is in a machine called a *tokamak*. This doughnut-shaped device was developed in the U.S.S.R. in the 1960s. Magnetic fields in a tokamak spin plasma in a circle. This will allow the plasma to be held together very tightly, which is necessary for nuclear fusion.

On the left-hand page is an artist's drawing of a tokamak fusion test reactor. The photograph below shows an actual tokamak fusion test reactor.

The Tokamak Fusion Test Reactor at Princeton University is one of the largest in the world. It will help develop the knowledge needed to build demonstration fusion power plants around the year 2000. The United States and other countries hope that commercial fusion reactors might start generating electricity between 2020 and 2030.

Princeton University

The fusion energy program will be long and costly. However, the end result would be a near endless source of power, since energy could be taken from water.

Thermo means heat. Nuclear fusion is called a *thermonuclear reaction* because of the very high temperatures needed to produce fusion. The hydrogen bomb is a thermonuclear weapon. Thus, nuclear fusion occurs when a hydrogen bomb explodes. The temperature inside these powerful weapons is about 10 million °C. An atomic bomb is exploded inside the hydrogen bomb to produce the temperatures needed to start nuclear fusion. Once ignited, the thermonuclear reaction occurs in less than .000001 second.

Hydrogen bombs of almost unlimited power can be built. Both the United States and the Soviet Union have thousands of nuclear weapons. Most people believe that if the two nations used these weapons fully in a war, life on earth could cease to exist.

On the right is a photograph of a test explosion of a nuclear weapon.

THE FUTURE OF NUCLEAR ENERGY

The future of nuclear energy is unclear. Concerns for safety, especially after the Three Mile Island accident, have slowed the development of nuclear power plants in the United States. The costs of building the plants have also risen to 2 to 3 billion dollars. By late 1981, plans to build new reactors had almost come to a halt.

In many other parts of the world, the use of nuclear energy is expanding rapidly. France and Japan are planning for nuclear power to provide most of their electricity in the future.

Research in the United States and abroad has shown ways to improve the efficiency of nuclear reactors. This will give us even more energy from fission. In addition, scientists and engineers have come up with ways to re-use some of the uranium 235 and plutonium that is mixed in with the nuclear waste. Recycling nuclear waste was forbidden by President Carter. He was afraid that dangerous plutonium could

At the left is an anti-nuclear demonstration.

fall into the hands of terrorists, who might build bombs. However, President Reagan decided to allow recycling again, in hopes that this would help to make nuclear plants more efficient and cheaper.

Uranium is a rare element worldwide. And only 7 out of every 1000 atoms of uranium can be used for fission in a nuclear reactor. These rare atoms are the isotope U-235. The more common U-238 is not readily fissionable. However, when "blanketed" around the core of a breeder reactor, U-238 can be changed into plutonium 239, which is more fissionable. Therefore, while the breeder reactor is generating electricity, it makes more fuel than it uses. In 12 to 15 years a breeder reactor could make enough plutonium to refuel itself and another reactor the same size. A number of nations are developing breeder reactors. In the United States, the Clinch River Breeder Reactor has been planned for construction near Oak Ridge, Tennessee. However, some people don't want breeder reactors to be built because they make plutonium. Plutonium can be used to build powerful bombs.

Useful energy from nuclear fusion is also possible in the future. However, as described earlier, enormous problems still have to be solved before it can be used to generate electricity. Yet, the abundant source of fuel — water — appears to make the effort worthwhile. In addition, fusion reactors don't make radioactive wastes, since nuclei don't break up as in the fission process. There would, therefore, be no worries about dangerous wastes.

In spite of all the problems and concerns with nuclear energy, it remains a powerful and reliable source of energy. What do you think about nuclear energy? Do the benefits of nuclear energy outweigh the problems? Should we develop breeder reactors? Our answer to the question of nuclear power may decide the quality of our future life.

The photograph below is of a reactor that is used to test nuclear fuel and components for irradiation—exposure to radiation. The reactor containment building, in the center, is surrounded by dump heat exchangers. Samples of nuclear fuels and other materials are placed in the core to determine their reaction to being exposed to radiation.

U.S. Department of Energy

This map of the world shows the concentration of commercial nuclear power plants that had been completed or were under construction in the early 1980s.

PRONUNCIATION GUIDE

These symbols have the same sound as the darker letters in the sample words.

ə	balloon, ago
a	map, have
ä	father, car
b	ball, rib
d	did, add
e	bell, get
ē	keen, leap
f	fan, soft
g	good, big
h	hurt, ahead
i	rip, ill
ī	side, sky
j	join, germ
k	king, ask
l	let, cool
m	man, same
n	no, turn
ō	cone, know
ȯ	all, saw
p	part, scrap
r	root, tire
s	so, press
sh	shoot, machine
t	to, stand
ü	pool, lose
u̇	put, book
v	view, give
w	wood, glowing
y	yes, year
′	accent

GLOSSARY

These words are defined the way they are used in the book.

alpha particle (al′ fə pärt′ i kəl) a positively charged particle given out by an atom during radioactive decay

atom (at′ əm) the basic part of all matter; the smallest part of an element that has all the chemical properties of that element

atomic number (ə täm′ ik nəm′ bər) the number of protons in the nucleus of an atom. All atoms of an element have the same atomic number

beta particle (bāt′ə pärt′ i kəl) a negatively charged particle given out by an atom during radioactive decay

coolant (kü′ lənt) a fluid, usually water, used to cool a nuclear reactor and carry heat. The water also moderates, or slows down, the fissioning of neutrons

critical mass (krit′ i kəl mas) the smallest amount of fuel necessary to sustain a chain reaction

deuterium (dü tir′ ē əm) a form of hydrogen that is twice as heavy as normal hydrogen

electron (i lek′ trän) a basic particle that orbits the nucleus of an atom and has a negative charge

fission (fish′ ən) the splitting or breaking apart of a heavy atom into two or more new atoms

fusion (fyü′ zhən) the uniting of two or more atomic nuclei to form one nucleus and release energy

gamma ray (gam′ ə rā) a form of high energy radiation given out by the nucleus of an atom

isotopes (ī′ sə tōps) different forms of the same chemical element which have different numbers of neutrons in the nucleus

mass number (mas′ nəm′ bər) the sum of the protons and neutrons in the nucleus of an atom

millirem (mil′ ə rem) a basic unit of radiation exposure

neutron (nü′ trän) an uncharged particle in the nucleus of an atom

nucleus (nü′ klē əs) the core or center of an atom, containing protons and, usually, neutrons

plasma (plaz′ mə) a collection of charged atomic particles

radioactivity (rād ē ō ak tiv′ ə tē) the property that some elements, such as uranium, have of giving out alpha, beta, or gamma rays

tokamak (tōk′ ə mak) a doughnut-shaped device that holds plasma tightly together in a fusion reactor

turbine (tər′ bən) an engine that is powered by spinning blades

uranium (yü rā′ nē əm) a heavy radioactive element, the basic fuel of a nuclear reactor

INDEX

gamma radiation, 10
gamma ray, 10, 11
Geiger counter, 10, 16
half-life, 11, 32
Hiroshima (Japan), 17
hydrogen bomb, 38
isotope, 8, 10, 11, 32
mass, 7
mass number, 7-8
matter, 13
Nagasaki, (Japan), 17
Nautilus, 25
natural gas, 5, 19
neutron, 6, 7, 8, 14-15, 22
nucleus, 6-7, 8-10
nuclear energy, definition of, 5-6
nuclear fission, 14, 15, 17, 22, 27
    32, 41
  definition of, 14
nuclear fusion, 35, 36, 37, 38, 42
nuclear power plant, 19, 27, 28
    29-31, 32, 41
  accidents in, 29-31
nuclear reactor, 22-25, 27, 32, 37,
    41
  boiling water, 23
  fuel assembly, 32
  pressurized water, 23-25
Nuclear Regulatory Commission, 32
nuclear waste, 29, 32, 41-42
nuclear weapons, 38
oil, 5, 19
plasma, 36, 37
  definition of, 36
plutonium, 32, 41, 42

plutonium 239, 42
proton, 6, 7, 8
radiation sickness, 10
radioactive decay, 10-11
radioactivity, 8-10, 11, 22, 28
    29, 32
  control of, 27-28
  dangers of, 28-29
Rutherford, Ernest, 10
thermonuclear reaction, 38
Three Mile Island, 30, 41
tokamak, 37
Tokamak Fusion Test Reactor, 37
tritium, 35-36
turbine, 36
University of Chicago, 16
uranium, 8, 19-20, 21-22, 23, 32, 42
  mining process, 20
uranium 235 (U-235), 8, 13, 14-15, 16,
    19, 20, 23, 27, 41, 42
uranium 238 (U-238), 8, 11, 20, 42
Windscale nuclear reactor, 29
wood, 5
X ray, 10